DIABETES

In memory of Robert Jodoin,
who inspired the Know What to Eat series.

Note
This publication was written by a registered dietitian to provide insights into better eating habits to promote health and wellness. It does not provide a cure for any specific ailment or condition and is not a substitute for the advice and/or treatment given by a licensed physician.

First published in French in 2013 by Les Publications Modus Vivendi Inc. under the title *Diabète*.
© Alexandra Leduc and Les Publications Modus Vivendi Inc., 2016

MODUS VIVENDI PUBLISHING
55 Jean-Talon Street West
Montreal, Quebec H2R 2W8
CANADA

modusvivendipublishing.com

Publisher: Marc G. Alain
Editorial director: Isabelle Jodoin
Editorial assistant and copy editor: Nolwenn Gouezel
English-language editor: Carol Sherman
Translator: Rhonda Mullins
Proofreader: Maeve Haldane
Graphic designers: Émilie Houle and Gabrielle Lecomte
Food photographer: André Noël
Food stylist: Gabrielle Dalessandro
Author's photographer: André Noël
Additional food photography:
Pages 63, 122 and 127: Dreamstime.com
Additional photography:
Pages 5, 6, 8, 12, 14, 16, 17, 21, 23, 25, 27, 35 to 55, 58, 61, 64, 68, 78, 85, 89, 90, 92, 94, 97, 106, 111, 120, 123, 130 and 134: Dreamstime.com
Page 133: iStock

ISBN: 978-1-77286-004-7 (PAPERBACK)

ISBN: 978-1-77286-005-4 (PDF)
ISBN: 978-1-77286-006-1(EPUB)
ISBN: 978-1-77286-007-8 (KINDLE)

Legal deposit – Bibliothèque et Archives nationales du Québec, 2016
Legal deposit – Library and Archives Canada, 2016

We gratefully acknowledge the financial support of the Government of Canada through the Canada Book Fund (CBF) for our publishing activities.

Government of Quebec – Tax Credit for Book Publishing – Program administered by SODEC

Printed in Canada

KNOW WHAT TO EAT

DIABETES

21 DAYS OF MENUS

Alexandra Leduc, RD

MODUS VIVENDI

CONTENTS

INTRODUCTION

The goal of this book is to provide tools for eating right and better controlling diabetes.

While this book is designed for diabetics, the recommendations and recipes can be used by anyone for diabetes prevention.

This book is not a replacement for the expertise of a dietitian, who will be able to assess your needs, habits and level of physical activity and take into account your likes and dislikes to come up with a personalized nutrition program.

This program, combined with medication and physical activity, will help you better control your diabetes. Eating a more balanced diet will help reduce the risk of complications from diabetes.

DIABETES

Diabetes is a chronic illness. It is a metabolic disorder that leads to the poor management of carbohydrates (sugars) because of a problem with the production of insulin, insulin resistance or the two combined.

There are two types of diabetes.

TYPE 1 DIABETES

Better known as juvenile diabetes, type 1 diabetes appears in childhood or adolescence and is characterized by the body producing little or no insulin. This type of diabetes cannot be prevented, and the only treatment is insulin injections.

TYPE 2 DIABETES

With type 2 diabetes, there is poor insulin flow, cell resistance to insulin or both. Onset occurs later in life, often after the age of 40. Ninety percent of diabetics suffer from this form of diabetes. A genetic predisposition, a sedentary lifestyle, obesity and food rich in fat and concentrated sugars can contribute to its onset.

Type 2 diabetes can be controlled by making lifestyle improvements, including a balanced diet, regular physical activity and effective stress management, as well as appropriate medication. A healthy lifestyle can reduce the risk of type 2 diabetes or delay its onset.

BIOLOGY 101

To understand diabetes, we need to know a bit about how the human body normally works. The body's main source of fuel is carbohydrates, which is a synonym for sugars. Carbohydrates come from food such as fruit, grains, dairy products and certain foods high in sugar, such as honey, jam and packaged deserts.

During digestion, carbohydrates are broken down into a molecule called glucose. Glucose is absorbed in the blood after digestion. As a result, blood glucose (the level of sugar in the blood) increases after eating, something that applies to everyone.

Cells need glucose to do their job. So the pancreas, located near the stomach, secretes insulin (a hormone) when blood sugar is high to get the sugar to the cells. Insulin is like a key that unlocks the cells to let in the sugar needed for the body's energy process. It also stabilizes sugar levels in the blood.

In diabetics, insulin is not secreted in sufficient quantities or is not as effective. As a result, it doesn't properly play its role as a key to reduce the blood sugar levels. Hyperglycemia results (a blood sugar level that is higher than normal), which is typical of type 2 diabetes.

If diabetes is not monitored and treated appropriately, in the long term it can cause serious complications for different parts of the body.

COMPLICATIONS OF DIABETES

Eyes: cataracts, glaucoma, vision loss.

Nerves: neuropathy (ailment that affects the nerves and causes tingling, loss of sensation and pain, often in the extremities).

Immune system: sensitivity to infections and poor healing that can result in ulcers and even gangrene that requires amputation.

Kidneys: nephropathy (progressive deterioration of kidneys that can lead to kidney failure, which is irreversible).

Heart: greater risk of heart attack.

Brain: greater risk of stroke.

CONTROLLING BLOOD SUGAR

Reading blood sugar levels teaches you how your body reacts to ingesting carbohydrates and to other influences.

Tracking blood sugar using a blood glucose monitor allows you to adjust your habits (food, insulin injections, physical activity) to regulate your sugar levels as much as possible and to quickly notify your doctor if your blood sugar is difficult to control.

Target blood sugar levels for someone suffering from diabetes
Fasting or before a meal 72 to 126 mg/dl* (4 to 7 mmol/l)**
Two hours after the start of a meal 90 to 180 mg/dl (5 to 10 mmol/l)

*mg/dl = milligrams per deciliter

**mmol/l = millimoles per liter

Proper control of blood sugar reduces the risk of complications. You should take your blood sugar levels based on the recommendations of your doctor or dietitian, or if you feel discomfort that could be a symptom of hypoglycemia or hyperglycemia.

HYPOGLYCEMIA

Hypoglycemia is a drop in the blood sugar level below normal. It can be dangerous to the point of causing a diabetic coma. Hypoglycemia can be brought on by medication, overly intense physical activity or a poorly balanced diet. It is important to consult your doctor or dietitian if you are regularly hypoglycemic.

Symptoms of hypoglycemia

- Reduced energy, weakness
- Agitation
- Sweating
- Headaches
- Heart palpitations
- Dizziness, drowsiness
- Incoherent speech

HYPERGLYCEMIA

Hyperglycemia is an increase in blood sugar levels above normal.

Symptoms of hyperglycemia

- Excessive urination
- Increased thirst and hunger
- Fatigue
- Excessive drowsiness
- Blurred vision

DAILY DIETARY
Recommendations

Diabetes is a complex chronic illness that, contrary to popular belief, does not develop solely in people who eat too much sugary food. You don't have to eliminate natural sugars from your diet, which would be detrimental to your health and make it harder to control your blood sugar.

The following are the main dietary recommendations to help balance your diet and better manage your diabetes. It is also a good idea to be under a dietitian's care to have a custom diet plan developed that suits not only your pace, your schedule and your food preferences, but also your level of physical activity and medication.

RECOMMENDATIONS:

1. Eat at regular times
2. Eat balanced meals
3. Choose natural carbohydrates
4. Eat more fiber
5. Vary your diet
6. Choose good fats
7. Avoid refined sugars
8. Limit alcohol consumption
9. Read labels

1 EAT AT REGULAR TIMES

Eating meals at regular times is important for helping your medication do its job. The body must not be in a fasting state (going several hours without a meal) to avoid increasing blood sugar imbalances. Meals should be spaced every four to six hours, with two hours between a meal and a snack. So your day should include at least three meals and snacks as needed (based on the recommendations of your dietitian or depending on how hungry you are).

2 EAT BALANCED MEALS

At every meal, fill a quarter of your plate with a source of protein that is low in fat. That is sufficient to give you the protein and nutrients you need.

Fill another quarter of your plate with whole-grain products and starchy foods (see the list on page 19).

Fill the remaining half of your plate with vegetables in different forms (raw vegetables, soups, salads, steamed vegetables, etc.).

Aim for a balanced plate during the two main meals (lunch and dinner). It's a simple way of better controlling your diabetes.

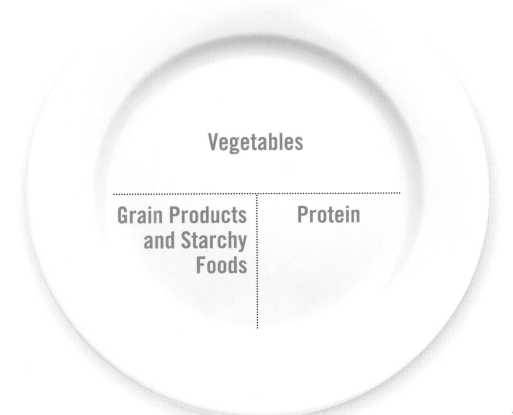

Vegetables

Grain Products and Starchy Foods

Protein

3 CHOOSE NATURAL CARBOHYDRATES

It is true that carbohydrates increase blood sugar, but it's important to understand that this is a perfectly normal reaction. Too often, people with diabetes eliminate carbohydrates from their diet, thinking this will help control the disease. On the contrary, proper control of diabetes depends on the right choice of carbohydrates. And you can't live without carbohydrates, because they are your brain's main source of energy.

Consume 2 to 5 servings of fruit, 6 to 10 servings of grain products and starchy foods and 2 to 4 servings of dairy products, per day.

Here are good sources of carbohydrates to include in your diet.

FRUIT – 2 to 5 servings per day

1 serving equals:

- 1 medium-sized fruit (orange, peach, apple, pear, etc.)
- ½ banana or ½ grapefruit
- 2 kiwis, 2 plums or 2 clementines
- 3 prunes
- 15 large grapes
- 1 cup (250 ml) cantaloupe, honeydew melon, blackberries
- 2 cups (500 ml) whole strawberries
- 2 tbsp raisins
- ½ cup (125 ml) fruit in pieces or fruit sauce with no added sugar
- ½ cup (125 ml) 100% fruit juice with no sugar added

GRAIN PRODUCTS AND STARCHY FOODS – 6 to 10 servings per day

1 serving equals:

- 1 slice whole-grain bread
- ½ whole-grain pita bread or ½ whole-grain hamburger bun
- 2 pieces Melba toast
- ½ medium-sized potato (ideally with peel)
- ½ cup (125 ml) mashed potatoes
- ⅓ cup (80 ml) cooked rice, barley or couscous
- ⅓ cup (80 ml) cooked whole wheat pasta
- ½ cup (125 ml) corn kernels or ½ corn on the cob
- ½ cup (125 ml) cooked legumes (baked beans, lentils, etc.)
- ⅓ cup (80 ml) cooked chickpeas
- ½ cup (125 ml) low-sugar breakfast cereal, with at least 2 g of fiber per serving

DAIRY PRODUCTS – 2 to 4 servings per day

1 serving equals:

- 1 cup (250 ml) milk
- 1 cup (250 ml) enriched plain soy milk
- ¾ cup (175 ml) plain yogurt
- 2 3.5 oz (100 g) container (⅔ cup/160 ml) fruit or flavored yogurt, fat-free with no added sugar
- 1 3.5 oz (100 g) container (⅓ cup/80 ml) fruit or flavored yogurt (vanilla, coffee, etc.)

4 EAT MORE FIBER

A diet rich in fiber is essential if you have diabetes. Fiber is found in whole-grain products, fruit, vegetables, nuts and legumes. Fiber acts mechanically by swelling in the stomach and increasing the digestion time for meals. A meal that is digested more slowly allows for slower absorption of dietary carbohydrates (sugars). In other words, fiber helps control blood sugar. Studies have shown its benefits in the diabetic diet.

Tips for increasing fiber in your diet

- Choose whole wheat pasta or, if you don't like it, make half white pasta and half whole wheat pasta.

- Choose long-grain white rice or brown rice that contains at least 2 g of fiber per ½ cup (125 ml).

- Eat at least four servings of vegetables daily.

- Eat a handful of nuts or almonds daily.

- Add ground flaxseeds, chia seeds, wheat germ, oat bran or All-Bran or All-Bran Buds to your yogurt, pancake batter, homemade muffins, cake mixes and breakfast cereal.

5 VARY YOUR DIET

For diabetics, and for the population in general, food variety and quality is essential. The more varied your diet, the greater the intake of vitamins and minerals necessary for good health. Variety also reduces routine and increases the pleasure of eating.

Here are a few ideas for diversifying your choices.

FRUIT

Berries, oranges, melons, cantaloupes, apples, pears, bananas, grapes, cranberries, plums, prunes, nectarines, peaches, cherries, dates, apricots, grapefruit, pineapple, kiwis, pomegranates, figs, mangos.

VEGETABLES

Asparagus, beets, zucchini, spaghetti squash, sweet potato, celeriac, radishes, avocado, olives, squash, spinach, cabbage, bok choy, purple cauliflower, fennel, broccoflower, blue potatoes.

GRAIN PRODUCTS

Quinoa, couscous, bulgur, barley, oats, wheat bran, buckwheat, oat bran, whole wheat pasta, millet, whole-grain bread, quinoa pasta, rice pasta, whole wheat pasta.

DAIRY AND SUBSTITUTES

Milk, yogurt, cheese, soy milk, almond milk.

Tips for diversifying your intake of dairy products

- Make dairy desserts, such as tapioca, rice pudding and milkshakes.

- Eat yogurt and cheese as a snack and for dessert.

- Serve vegetables and your favorite dishes au gratin with different sorts of cheese that is 20% M.F. or less.

- Drink soy milk enriched with calcium and vitamin D, or choose soy desserts.

SOURCES OF PROTEIN

Choose a variety of animal- and plant-based proteins. Here are a few examples from each category.

Lean red meat: extra-lean ground beef, veal, pork

Game: bison, venison, moose, caribou

Poultry: chicken, duck, turkey

Fish: salmon, trout, tuna, sole, tilapia

Seafood: shrimp, scallops, oysters, lobster, crab

Legumes: red, black or white beans, lentils, lima beans, lupin beans, chickpeas

Nuts and grains: almonds, hazelnuts, Brazil nuts, nut butters, natural peanut butter, soybean seeds, sunflower seeds, flaxseeds, chia seeds

Soy: silken tofu, regular tofu, edamame

Eggs

6 CHOOSE GOOD FATS

Diabetes increases the risk of heart disease. This is why it is important to choose good fats (unsaturated fats) and reduce sources of saturated fats (less good fats).

UNSATURATED FATS (GOOD FATS)

Fatty fish: salmon, trout, sardines, herring

Nuts: walnuts, Brazil nuts, pecans, almonds, hazelnuts

Seeds: flax, chia, soybean, sunflower

Oils: canola, sunflower, olive, grapeseed

Non-hydrogenated margarine

Tofu and soy products

UNSATURATED AND TRANS FATS (LESS GOOD FATS)

Butter

Meat and cold cuts

Fatty dairy products: cheese, cream, 3.25% M.F. milk

Cookies, cakes, crackers, store-bought muffins

7 AVOID REFINED SUGARS

Unlike fiber, foods with refined sugars make it harder to control blood sugar. These sugars are quickly digested and, in turn, quickly increase blood sugar. Plus they have little nutritional value. Sweet, nutrition-poor foods (see the list below) should be eaten only occasionally and in very small quantities.

- White sliced bread, white hamburger and hot dog buns, white pasta, white rice
- Pizza dough, pastries, pie, cake, candies, chocolate candy bars, cookies, ice cream, popsicles
- White sugar
- Soft drinks, juice and fruit cocktails, chocolate milk
- Sugary breakfast cereals

It can be hard to make sense of it all. You don't necessarily need to eliminate all of these foods from your diet, but be aware that consuming them can make it harder to control your diabetes.

BE CAREFUL WITH SUGAR SUBSTITUTES

There are plenty of different artificial sweeteners on the market: Aspartame, sucralose, saccharine, cyclamate, etc.

However, these products are not recommended, because they can create sugar cravings. And the effects of artificial sweeteners on the human body are also not clear.

It's better to use regular sugar when cooking and simply use less of it, or to replace it with fruit or sources of natural sugar (honey, maple syrup, etc.). This will help get you used to a less sweet taste.

Tips for reducing refined sugars in your diet

- Cook whenever possible and cut the sugar called for in recipes by half.

- Cook with wholesome ingredients, such as vegetables, fruit and whole grains.

- Avoid store-bought desserts.

- Learn to read nutrition labels and look at the list of ingredients. Look for products that do not have sugar in the top three ingredients.

- Avoid the refined foods listed left.

- Use whole-grain products instead of refined grains.

- Don't add white sugar (or try to cut back gradually) to your cereal, coffee or tea.

- Opt for water, mineral water and unsweetened tea or coffee rather than juice or soft drinks, even if they are "diet."

8 LIMIT ALCOHOL CONSUMPTION

Alcohol increases the risk of hypoglycemia. To reduce this risk, it should be consumed with meals. Alcohol is not recommended for diabetics who have a hard time controlling their blood sugar. So it is better to have stable blood sugar before drinking alcohol occasionally.

1 drink	{	1 beer
		5 oz (150 ml) wine
		1.5 oz (45 ml) spirits

Women
Maximum of 1 drink daily
Maximum of 7 drinks weekly

Men
Maximum of 2 drinks daily
Maximum of 14 drinks weekly

9 READ LABELS

Here is what to look for on nutrition labels when shopping.

Nutrition Facts Per serving	
Amount	
Calories	423
Fat	15 g
Sodium	587 mg
Carbohydrate	45 g
Fiber	6 g
Protein	30 g

Carbohydrate (in grams): Indicates the total amount of carbohydrates, which includes fiber, sugar and starch (rarely indicated on the label).

Fiber (in grams): Dietary fiber has no effect on blood sugar, so it should be subtracted from total carbohydrates. The higher the fiber, the better the choice.

Sugar (in grams): Indicates the amount of sugar found naturally in fruit and milk, as well as added sugar (such as white sugar, brown sugar, honey and molasses). It is normal for a glass of milk to contain sugar (natural sugar). To find out whether food contains added sugar, read the list of ingredients and check whether it includes sugar, glucose, fructose, honey, maple syrup, brown sugar, corn syrup or brown rice syrup.

For diabetics, the total amount of carbohydrates on the label (minus the fiber) is the reference value for knowing what amount of carbohydrates will affect your blood sugar. Ask your dietitian for the amount of carbohydrates you should consume at each meal.

FOODS TO CHOOSE

Grain products
Whole-grain bread, whole wheat pasta, long-grain brown rice, whole wheat couscous, whole wheat flour, quinoa, barley, millet.

Legumes
Lentils, red beans, chickpeas, split peas, etc.

Fresh fruit
At least two servings per day.

Fish and seefood
At least twice a week.

Lean animal protein
Chicken, lean beef, eggs, pork.

Plant-based protein
Nuts, almonds, tofu, sunflower seeds, soybean seeds, walnuts, soy milk.

Vegetable oil
Olive oil, canola oil, sunflower oil.

Steamed or grilled dishes or dishes cooked en papillote

Homemade desserts with less sugar

Reduced-fat dairy products
1% M.F. milk, cheese that is 20% M.F. or less, yogurt.

FOODS TO AVOID

Refined sugar
White sugar, candy, jam, honey, pastry, ice cream, sorbet, candied fruit, cake, donuts, soft drinks, juice or fruit cocktail, cookies, sugary breakfast cereal, pizza dough, white bread, white pasta, maple syrup, chocolate.

Animal fat
Butter, thick crème fraîche, lard, cheese with more than 20% M.F., cold cuts, fatty meats, 35% M.F. cream.

Foods high in salt
Cold cuts, cocktail biscuits, canned soup, vegetable juice, marinades.

Foods high in fat
Cold cuts, pastry, pâté, pie, cream-based sauces, chips, breaded foods.

Alcohol
Only drink in moderation, if your blood sugar is under control.

21 DAYS
OF MENUS

The following menus were designed to ensure you have all the nutrients, carbohydrates and energy you need for the day. The meals and snacks are inter-changeable between days. If you aren't hungry between meals, you can eat your snack as dessert.

You should also eat to satisfy your hunger. Try to eat everything on your plate, but don't force yourself to finish if you are no longer hungry.

If you have a small appetite, you should be sure to consume a variety of foods every day from the three groups (protein, starch and vegetables) at every meal.

Plan your week. In the menus, lunch is generally leftovers from the night before. When you cook, you can double servings as needed to have leftovers the next day.

If you have questions or your blood sugar is still hard to control, even when you follow the menus, you should see a dietitian who will be able to adapt the menus and serving sizes to your needs.

DAY 1

BREAKFAST..

Oatmeal with Fruit (p. 58)

Snack
½ banana

LUNCH...

Quick Pasta Salad (p. 75)

Snack
1 Blueberry Muffin (p. 118)

DINNER...

Mustard Salmon (p. 76)

Snack
1 fruit yogurt
4 social tea biscuits

BREAKFAST

1 or 2 slices whole wheat toast
1 oz (30 g) cheese
½ cup (125 ml) 100% pure orange juice

Snack
15 green or red grapes

LUNCH

Mustard Salmon (p. 76)

Snack
½ cup (125 ml) Orange Tapioca
(p. 120)

DINNER

Colorful Bell Pepper Fajitas (p. 78)

Snack
1 slice whole-grain toast
1 tbsp natural peanut butter

DAY 3

BREAKFAST..

1 plain yogurt
½ cup (125 ml) Apple Granola (p. 61)
½ cup (125 ml) fresh fruit

> **Snack**
> ½ cup (125 ml) apple sauce,
> no added sugar

LUNCH..

Colorful Bell Pepper Fajitas (p. 78)

> **Snack**
> 1 cup (250 ml) low-sodium
> vegetable juice
> 4 crackers

DINNER..

Chickpea Croquettes with Cucumber Tomato Salad (p. 80)

> **Snack**
> 1 cup (250 ml) milk

DAY 4

BREAKFAST

1 Energy 101 Smoothie (p. 62)

Snack
½ banana

LUNCH

Chickpea Croquettes with Cucumber Tomato Salad (p. 80)

Snack
1 Blueberry Muffin (p. 118)

DINNER

Frittata (p. 82)

Snack
1 fruit yogurt
4 social tea biscuits

DAY 5

BREAKFAST

¾ cup (180 ml) high-fiber cereal
½ cup (125 ml) milk
1 piece of fruit

Snack
15 red or green grapes

LUNCH

Frittata (p. 82)

Snack
½ cup (125 ml) Orange Tapioca
(p. 120)

DINNER

Lemony Thyme Pork and Couscous (p. 85)

Snack
1 oz (30 g) cheese
4 crackers

DAY 6

BREAKFAST..

2 Fluffy Blueberry Pancakes (p. 64)

Snack
½ cup (125 ml) apple sauce,
no sugar added

LUNCH..

Lemony Thyme Pork and Couscous (p. 85)

Snack
1 fruit yogurt

DINNER..

Cajun Chicken Croquettes with Vegetable Salad (p. 86)

Snack
2 cups (500 ml) homemade popcorn
1 cup (250 ml) milk

DAY 7

BREAKFAST...

Breakfast Omelet (p.66)

Snack
½ cup (125 ml) Orange Tapioca
(p. 120)

LUNCH...

Cajun Chicken Croquettes with Vegetable Salad (p. 86)

Snack
1 Blueberry Muffin (p. 118)

DINNER...

Rice with Corn Salsa (p. 89)

Snack
1 cup (250 ml) milk

DAY 8

BREAKFAST

1 plain yogurt
½ cup (125 ml) Apple Granola (p. 61)
½ cup (125 ml) fresh fruit

Snack
15 red or green grapes

LUNCH

Rice with Corn Salsa (p. 89)

Snack
1 cup (250 ml) milk

DINNER

Spaghetti with Ground Pork (p. 90)

Snack
1 slice whole-grain toast
1 tbsp natural peanut butter

DAY 9

BREAKFAST

1 Carrot Yogurt Muffin (p. 68)
1 cup (250 ml) milk

Snack
1 apple
10 almonds

LUNCH

Spaghetti with Ground Pork (p. 90)

Snack
1 cup (250 ml) Peach Crisp (p. 123)

DINNER

Spinach Quiche with Green Salad (p. 92)

Snack
½ cup high-fiber cereal
½ cup (125 ml) milk

DAY 10

BREAKFAST

Raspberry Oatmeal Smoothie (p. 63)
10 almonds

Snack
½ cup (125 ml) fruit salad

LUNCH

Spinach Quiche with Green Salad (p. 92)

Snack
1 Carrot Yogurt Muffin (p. 68)

DINNER

Hearty Beef Soup (p. 94)

Snack
1 cup (250 ml) milk

DAY 11

BREAKFAST

1 whole wheat English muffin
1 tbsp natural peanut butter
½ cup (125 ml) 100% pure orange juice

Snack
Hummus and raw vegetables

LUNCH

Hearty Beef Soup (p. 94)

Snack
15 red or green grapes
1 oz (30 g) cheese

DINNER

Asian Shrimp (p. 97)

Snack
1 yogurt
4 social tea biscuits

DAY 12

BREAKFAST..

¾ cup (180 ml) cottage cheese
½ cup (125 ml) fresh fruit
1 slice whole-grain bread

Snack
1 cup (250 ml) milk

LUNCH..

Asian Shrimp (p. 97)

Snack
1 cup (250 ml) Peach Crisp (p. 123)

DINNER..

Salmon Burger (p. 98)

Snack
1 slice whole-grain toast
1 oz (30 g) cheese

DAY 13

BREAKFAST

Egg on Toasty Bread (p. 70)
1 piece fruit

Snack
½ cup (125 ml) fruit salad

LUNCH

Salmon Burger (p. 98)

Snack
1 fruit yogurt

DINNER

Orange Beef (p. 100)

Snack
½ cup (125 ml) milk
½ cup (125 ml) high-fiber cereal

DAY 14

BREAKFAST

¾ cup (180 ml) high-fiber cereal
½ cup (125 ml) milk
1 piece fruit

Snack
1 Carrot Yogurt Muffin (p. 68)

LUNCH

Orange Beef (p. 100)

Snack
½ cup (125 ml) fruit salad

DINNER

Maple Chicken Brochette (p. 102)

Snack
2 cups (500 ml) homemade popcorn
1 cup (250 ml) milk

DAY 15

BREAKFAST

1 or 2 pieces toasted oat bread
1 egg
½ cup (125 ml) 100% pure orange juice

Snack
1 fruit yogurt

LUNCH

Maple Chicken Brochette (p. 102)

Snack
1 Oatmeal Date Cookie (p. 124)

DINNER

Mexican Soup with Pita Chips (p. 105)

Snack
1 cup (250 ml) milk

DAY 16

BREAKFAST

¾ cup (180 ml) cottage cheese
½ cup (125 ml) fresh fruit
1 slice whole-grain bread

Snack
½ cup (125 ml) pineapple

LUNCH

Mexican Soup with Pita Chips (p. 105)

Snack
1 Lemon Pudding (p. 126)

DINNER

Fruity Chicken and Quinoa Salad (p. 106)

Snack
½ cup (125 ml) high-fiber cereal
½ cup (125 m) milk

DAY 17

BREAKFAST...

1 whole wheat English muffin
1 tbsp natural peanut butter

Snack	
1 apple 10 almonds	

LUNCH..

Fruity Chicken and Quinoa Salad (p. 106)

Snack	
1 fruit yogurt	

DINNER......................................

Pasta Shells with Olives, Tuna and Tomatoes (p. 108)

Snack	
½ cup (125 ml) milk 1 Oatmeal Date Cookie (p. 124)	

DAY 18

BREAKFAST..

¾ cup (180 ml) high-fiber cereal
½ cup (125 ml) milk

Snack
½ cup (125 ml) pineapple

LUNCH..

Pasta Shells with Olives, Tuna and Tomatoes (p. 108)

Snack
1 Lemon Pudding (p. 126)

DINNER..

Egg Burger (p. 111)
1 cup (250 ml) milk

Snack
1 slice whole-grain toast
1 tbsp natural peanut butter

DAY 19

BREAKFAST

1 Carrot Yogurt Muffin (p. 68)
1 cup (250 ml) milk

Snack
1 cup (250 ml) apple sauce,
no sugar added

LUNCH

Egg Burger (p. 111)
1 cup (250 ml) milk

Snack
4 crackers
1 cup (250 ml) low-sodium
vegetable juice

DINNER

Breaded Pork Chop with Vegetable Pasta (p. 112)

Snack
1 piece fruit
10 almonds

DAY 20

BREAKFAST......................................

Oatmeal with Fruit (p. 58)

Snack
½ cup (125 ml) fruit salad

LUNCH......................................

Breaded Pork Chop with Vegetable Pasta (p. 112)

Snack
1 fruit yogurt

DINNER......................................

Sole en Papillote (p. 114)

Snack
1 Lemon Pudding (p. 126)

DAY 21

BREAKFAST..

Cinnamon French Toast (p. 72)
1 cup (250 ml) milk

Snack
1 Lemon Pudding (p. 126)

LUNCH..

Sole en Papillote (p. 114)

Snack
½ cup (125 ml) pineapple

DINNER..

Pita Pizza (p. 116)

Snack
½ cup (125 ml) high-fiber cereal
½ cup (125 ml) milk

RECIPES
36 HEALTHY IDEAS

Here are 36 healthy recipes that are simple to prepare. You will also find DIABETES INFO boxes with information about the impact of certain foods on your health and on controlling diabetes.

OATMEAL
with Fruit

1 serving • PREPARATION: 5 minutes • COOKING TIME: 2 to 3 minutes

INGREDIENTS

½ cup (125 ml) milk

⅓ cup (80 ml) old-fashioned rolled oats

10 almonds or other nuts

1 tsp maple syrup

¼ tsp ground cinnamon

½ cup (125 ml) raspberries or ½ sliced banana

METHOD

In a microwave-safe bowl, combine milk and oats.

Heat 2 to 3 minutes in microwave, stirring every minute.

Add almonds, maple syrup, cinnamon and fruit.

Stir and serve.

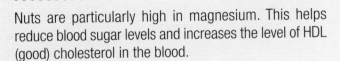

DIABETES INFO

Nuts are particularly high in magnesium. This helps reduce blood sugar levels and increases the level of HDL (good) cholesterol in the blood.

Nutrition Facts Per serving	
Amount	
Calories	280
Fat	10 g
Sodium	60 mg
Carbohydrate	40 g
Fiber	8 g
Protein	11 g

16 servings of ½ cup (125 ml) • PREPARATION: 5 minutes • COOKING TIME: 25 to 30 minutes

METHOD

Position rack in middle of oven and preheat to 350ºF (180ºC). Line a baking sheet with parchment paper.

In a large bowl, combine oats, almonds, apple sauce, honey and egg.

Spread mixture on prepared baking sheet.

Bake mixture in middle of preheated oven for 25 to 30 minutes, stirring every 5 minutes, until golden.

Once mixture is ready, add raisins and let cool before eating.

. . . .

TIP

For a complete meal, combine granola with fruits and 1 cup (250 ml) of plain yogurt.

INGREDIENTS

3 cups (750 ml) old-fashioned rolled oats

1 cup (250 ml) flaked almonds or other nuts

½ cup (125 ml) apple sauce, with no sugar added

¼ cup (60 ml) honey

1 egg

1 cup (250 ml) raisins

Nutrition Facts Per serving	
Amount	
Calories	123
Fat	4 g
Sodium	5 mg
Carbohydrate	21 g
Fiber	2.5 g
Protein	3 g

DIABETES INFO

Oats are very high in soluble fibers, including beta glucan, a type of fiber known to help regulate blood sugar levels. Regular consumption of oats and oat bran is recommended.

ENERGY

101 Smoothies

2 servings • PREPARATION: 5 minutes

INGREDIENTS

1 cup (250 ml) silken tofu

1 cup (250 ml) diced pineapple (fresh or canned)

1 cup (250 ml) milk

1 tbsp maple syrup

METHOD

In a food processor, combine all ingredients and purée until smooth.

Nutrition Facts	
Per serving	
Amount	
Calories	168
Fat	4 g
Sodium	62 mg
Carbohydrate	26 g
Fiber	1 g
Protein	9 g

RASPBERRY OATMEAL
Smoothie

1 serving • PREPARATION: 5 minutes

METHOD

In a food processor, combine all ingredients and mix.

INGREDIENTS

¾ cup (180 ml) milk

½ cup (125 ml) frozen raspberries

¼ cup (60 ml) quick-cooking rolled oats

1 tsp honey

Nutrition Facts Per serving	
Amount	
Calories	188
Fat	3 g
Sodium	86 mg
Carbohydrate	32 g
Fiber	5 g
Protein	9 g

FLUFFY BLUEBERRY
Pancakes

4 servings of 2 pancakes • PREPARATION: 10 minutes • COOKING TIME: 20 minutes

INGREDIENTS

1 cup (250 ml) unbleached all-purpose flour

1 cup (250 ml) whole wheat flour

2 tbsp brown sugar

1 tbsp baking powder

1½ cups (375 ml) milk

3 eggs

1 tbsp canola oil

1½ cups (375 ml) frozen blueberries

METHOD

In a bowl, combine flours, brown sugar and baking powder.

In another bowl, using a fork, combine milk, eggs and oil.

Pour wet ingredients over dry and mix thoroughly.

Add blueberries and stir until well distributed throughout batter.

Heat a large lightly oiled skillet over medium heat and pour in batter to form two pancakes the size of a soup bowl.

Cook pancakes on both sides, 5 to 6 minutes, until golden. Repeat with remaining batter.

Serve 2 pancakes per person.

DIABETES INFO

• •

Varieties of red and blue berries contain natural compounds called anthocyanins. These pigments are antioxidants known to reduce damage to cells and aging tissue. Premature aging of tissue can result in kidney failure, vision problems and hardening of the arteries, complications commonly found among diabetics.

Nutrition Facts Per serving	
Amount	
Calories	360
Fat	9 g
Sodium	320 mg
Carbohydrate	55 g
Fiber	5 g
Protein	14 g

Omelet

4 servings • PREPARATION: 5 minutes • COOKING TIME: 10 minutes

INGREDIENTS

8 eggs

¼ cup (60 ml) milk

¼ cup (60 ml) any grated cheese

1 green onion, chopped

Salt and pepper

METHOD

In a bowl, using a fork, beat eggs and milk. Add remaining ingredients and incorporate.

Pour mixture into a lightly oiled nonstick skillet over medium heat. Cook 2 to 3 minutes and fold in half to finish cooking.

Cut omelet in four and serve one portion per person.

Serve with fruit or 1 or 2 slices whole wheat toast for a complete breakfast.

Nutrition Facts
Per serving

Amount	
Calories	188
Fat	13 g
Sodium	180 mg
Carbohydrate	2 g
Fiber	0 g
Protein	15 g

CARROT YOGURT
Muffins

12 muffins • PREPARATION: 10 minutes • COOKING TIME: 30 minutes

INGREDIENTS

1 cup (250 ml) unbleached all-purpose flour

1 cup (250 ml) old-fashioned rolled oats

¼ cup (60 ml) brown sugar

½ tsp ground cinnamon

2 tsp baking powder

¼ cup (60 ml) canola oil

2 eggs

1 cup (250 ml) plain yogurt

2 cups (500 ml) grated carrot

½ cup (125 ml) 100% pure orange juice

METHOD

Position rack in middle of oven and preheat to 350ºF (180ºC). Lightly oil a muffin tin.

In a large bowl, combine flour, oats, brown sugar, cinnamon and baking powder.

In a separate bowl, using a mixer, combine canola oil with eggs and yogurt. Add grated carrots with a spoon.

Gradually add wet ingredients to dry ingredients, alternating with orange juice. Combine well.

Pour batter into prepared muffin tin and bake in middle of preheated oven for 30 minutes until a toothpick inserted in the center comes out clean.

DIABETES INFO

Carrots are one of the richest sources of beta carotene (vitamin A), known to reduce the risk of vision problems, which are among the most common complications of diabetes.

Nutrition Facts Per serving	
Amount	
Calories	150
Fat	6 g
Sodium	90 mg
Carbohydrate	25 g
Fiber	2 g
Protein	4 g

EGG
on Toasty Bread

1 serving • PREPARATION: 10 minutes • COOKING TIME: 5 minutes

INGREDIENTS

4 cups (1 l) water

2 tbsp white vinegar

1 egg

2 slices whole-grain bread

Salt and pepper

½ tsp dried parsley

METHOD

Pour water and vinegar in a saucepan, bring to a boil, then reduce heat to simmer.

Crack egg in water and, using a spoon, gather white around yolk.

Cook for 5 minutes.

In the meantime, toast bread (see Tip).

Once egg is cooked, remove from water with a skimmer and place carefully on a paper towel. Then place on toasted bread. Season and sprinkle with dried parsley.

• • • • • • • • • • • • • •

TIP

If you like, before toasting the bread, use a large round cookie cutter or clean lid and cut out a circle from the center of the bread to the size of the egg.

Nutrition Facts Per serving	
Amount	
Calories	149
Fat	6 g
Sodium	204 mg
Carbohydrate	30 g
Fiber	4 g
Protein	10 g

CINNAMON
French Toast

4 servings • PREPARATION: 5 minutes • COOKING TIME: 5 minutes

INGREDIENTS

2 eggs

1 tbsp milk

1 tbsp brown sugar

1 tsp ground cinnamon

4 slices whole-grain bread

2 bananas

METHOD

In a bowl, combine eggs, milk, brown sugar and cinnamon.

Heat a lightly oiled or nonstick skillet over medium-high heat. Dip both sides of each slice of bread in mixture. Place in skillet and fry slices until golden brown on one side, then flip and brown the other side.

Serve each slice with ½ a banana.

Nutrition Facts
Per serving

Amount	
Calories	177
Fat	4 g
Sodium	178 mg
Carbohydrate	30 g
Fiber	4 g
Protein	8 g

QUICK PASTA
Salad

4 servings • PREPARATION: 10 minutes • COOKING TIME: 20 minutes

METHOD

Cook macaroni in boiling water.

Meanwhile, combine yogurt, mayonnaise, lemon juice, green onion, garlic powder, salt and pepper.

Drain cooked macaroni and add vegetables and sauce. Combine thoroughly.

Serve 1½ cups (375 ml) salad per person. Cut hard-boiled eggs in half and top salad with four halves per person.

. . . .

TIPS

- Use the pasta you have on hand.
- Add your favorite vegetables.
- Replace eggs with canned tuna or salmon, or cooked chiken or shrimps.

INGREDIENTS

1 cup (250 ml) uncooked whole wheat macaroni

2 tbsp plain yogurt

2 tbsp light mayonnaise

1 tsp lemon juice

1 green onion, chopped

1 tbsp garlic powder

Salt and pepper

2 cups (500 ml) broccoli pieces

2 bell peppers, chopped

8 hard-boiled eggs

Nutrition Facts	
Per serving	
Amount	
Calories	395
Fat	14 g
Sodium	195 mg
Carbohydrate	60 g
Fiber	8 g
Protein	23 g

MUSTARD
Salmon

4 servings • **PREPARATION:** 10 minutes • **COOKING TIME:** 25 to 30 minutes

INGREDIENTS

2 tbsp Dijon mustard

2 tbsp dried parsley

1 tsp garlic powder

4 small or 2 large salmon fillets

2 medium onions, chopped, divided

2 cups (500 ml) broccoli pieces

3 to 4 carrots, cut in rounds
(about 2 cups/500 ml)

1 tbsp canola oil

1½ cups (375 ml) long-grain rice

1 tbsp low-sodium chicken bouillon
powder

METHOD

Preheat oven to 350ºF (180ºC).

In a small bowl, combine Dijon mustard, parsley and garlic powder.

Brush salmon fillets with mustard mixture.

Place salmon fillets in an ovenproof dish and spread one of the chopped onions, broccoli and carrots over top.

Bake salmon in preheated oven 25 to 30 minutes, depending on size.

Meanwhile, in a saucepan, heat canola oil over high heat and sauté remaining onion for 2 minutes.

Add rice and cook with chicken bouillon in water, following directions on the rice package.

Serve one salmon filet, vegetables and 1 cup (250 ml) rice per person.

• • • • • • • • • • • • •

TIPS

- Cook a large amount of rice in advance and freeze in portions in a freezer-proof dish. You'll save time when a recipe calls for rice.
- Double the recipe to have leftovers for lunch, depending on the number of people in your household.

Nutrition Facts Per serving	
Amount	
Calories	550
Fat	17 g
Sodium	505 mg
Carbohydrate	60 g
Fiber	5 g
Protein	27 g

COLORFUL BELL PEPPER
Fajitas

4 servings • PREPARATION: 10 minutes • COOKING TIME: 15 minutes

INGREDIENTS

1½ tbsp canola oil

4 medium boneless skinless chicken breasts, cut in strips

1 tbsp garlic powder

1 tbsp paprika

1 tsp Cajun spice mix

1 red pepper, cut in strips

1 yellow pepper, cut in strips

4 large tortillas

1 cup (250 ml) chopped lettuce

½ cup (125 m) salsa
(ideally low sodium)

1 cup (250 ml) grated cheese
(ideally 20% M.F. or less)

METHOD

In a saucepan, heat canola oil over high heat. Add chicken strips and brown 2 minutes on each side. Reduce heat. Add garlic powder, paprika and Cajun spice mix to chicken. Combine well.

When chicken strips are almost cooked through, add peppers and continue cooking 3 to 4 minutes.

Warm tortillas in oven for 1 minute before serving.

Let everyone prepare their own fajita with chicken, pepper, lettuce, salsa and cheese to taste.

Serve with green salad.

Nutrition Facts Per serving	
Amount	
Calories	495
Fat	17 g
Sodium	298 mg
Carbohydrate	50 g
Fiber	4 g
Protein	35 g

DIABETES INFO

Eat plenty of brightly colored vegetables (such as broccoli, peppers and carrots).

CHICKPEA CROQUETTES
with Cucumber Tomato Salad

6 servings of 2 croquettes and 4 servings of salad • PREPARATION: 10 minutes • COOKING TIME: 20 minutes

INGREDIENTS

2 cans (each 19 oz/540 ml) chickpeas, rinsed and drained

1 cup (250 ml) breadcrumbs

2 eggs

1 cup (250 ml) grated cheese

1 green pepper, finely chopped

1 tbsp dried thyme

1 tbsp garlic powder

1 tbsp canola oil

Salt and pepper

For the Cucumber Tomato Salad

1 cucumber

3 tomatoes

2 tbsp olive oil

Balsamic vinegar

METHOD

Preheat oven to 350ºF (180ºC).

In a food processor, combine all ingredients for Chickpea Croquettes and purée until smooth.

Using your hands, shape croquettes into 12 balls (each about 2 inches/5 cm). Place on a baking sheet.

Bake in preheated oven for 10 minutes, flip croquettes and bake 10 minutes more.

Serve 2 croquettes per person with Cucumber Tomato Salad.

In a large bowl, combine peeled, diced cucumber, 3 diced tomatoes, olive oil and balsamic vinegar. Season to taste.

• • • • • • • • • • • • • •

VARIATION

Replace thyme and garlic powder with curry powder, cumin or coriander to give croquettes an Indian flavor.

TIPS

- Make extra croquettes and freeze them. You'll have them on hand for a quick, healthy meal.
- Cut cooled croquettes into strips and serve on a multigrain tortilla with fresh tomatoes, lettuce and Dijon mustard.

Nutrition Facts Per serving (croquettes and salad	
Amount	
Calories	455
Fat	18 g
Sodium	300 mg
Carbohydrate	55 g
Fiber	8 g
Protein	20 g

FRITTATA

INGREDIENTS

8 eggs

¼ cup (60 ml) milk

1 small onion, chopped

2 zucchini, chopped

2 cups (500 ml) baby spinach

½ cup (125 ml) grated cheese

2 tbsp garlic powder

1 tbsp dried parsley

1 tsp dried oregano

Black pepper to taste

3 cups (750 ml) cooked whole wheat spaghetti

Grated cheese to top

4 slices whole-grain bread

METHOD

Position rack in middle of oven and preheat to 350ºF (180ºC). Lightly grease a 9-inch (23 cm) ovenproof pie plate.

In a bowl, using a fork, beat eggs and milk.

Add chopped onion, zucchini, spinach, cheese and seasoning. Combine thoroughly.

Place cooked spaghetti in bottom of prepared pie plate and pour egg mixture over top. Sprinkle with grated cheese to bake au gratin.

Bake in middle of preheated oven, 30 to 40 minutes, until lightly browned and puffed.

Cut frittata in four and serve with a slice of whole-grain bread.

· · · · · · · · · · · · · · ·

TIP

This recipe is ideal for using leftover cooked pasta. You can even add leftover chicken.

Nutrition Facts
Per serving

Amount	
Calories	330
Fat	7 g
Sodium	366 mg
Carbohydrate	48 g
Fiber	7 g
Protein	22 g

LEMONY THYME
Pork

4 servings • PREPARATION: 10 minutes • COOKING TIME: 20 to 25 minutes

METHOD

Preheat oven to 350ºF (180ºC).

Remove any visible fat from pork tenderloin and brush with canola oil.

In a small bowl, combine lemon zest, thyme, salt and pepper. Use your hands to rub pork with spice mixture. Coat thoroughly.

Place pork tenderloin in an ovenproof dish and surround with chopped onion, broccoli pieces and mushrooms.

Bake in preheated oven, 20 to 25 minutes, until meat is cooked to your liking.

Meanwhile, pour dry couscous into a large bowl and add boiling water and chicken bouillon. Stir and let sit.

Serve pork with vegetables and about 1 cup (250 ml) couscous per person.

INGREDIENTS

2 small pork tenderloins

1 tbsp canola oil

Zest of 2 lemons

3 tbsp dried thyme

Salt and pepper

1 small onion, chopped

2 cups (500 ml) broccoli pieces

2 cups (500 ml) mushrooms
or your choice of vegetable

1½ cups (375 ml) whole wheat couscous

3 cups (750 ml) boiling water

1 tbsp low-sodium chicken bouillon powder

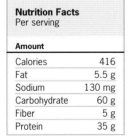

| Nutrition Facts | |
Per serving	
Amount	
Calories	416
Fat	5.5 g
Sodium	130 mg
Carbohydrate	60 g
Fiber	5 g
Protein	35 g

DIABETES INFO

Broccoli is rich in chromium, which plays an important long-term role in regulating blood sugar. Eating broccoli regularly, with its antioxidants and high-fiber content, is recommended for diabetics.

CAJUN CHICKEN CROQUETTES
with Vegetable Salad

4 servings • PREPARATION: 15 minutes • COOKING TIME: 20 minutes

INGREDIENTS

2 cups (500 ml) breadcrumbs

2 tbsp paprika

1 tbsp Cajun spice mix

1 tbsp chili powder

Salt and pepper

4 eggs

2 large boneless skinless chicken breasts, cut into large pieces

For the Vegetable Salad

1 cup (250 ml) each broccoli, cauliflower, zucchini, carrots or other vegetable

3 tbsp olive oil

2 tbsp lemon juice

Salt and pepper

METHOD

Preheat oven to 350°F (180°C).

In a plastic bag, combine breadcrumbs and seasoning.

Beat eggs and place in another plastic bag.

Dip chicken pieces in egg mixture, and then, using tongs, transfer to bag of breadcrumbs. Coat chicken well.

Place chicken pieces on a baking sheet and bake in preheated oven for 20 minutes.

Serve with Vegetable Salad or baked potato.

In a large bowl, combine broccoli pieces, cauliflower, zucchini and carrots (or other vegetable). Add olive oil and lemon juice. Season to taste.

Nutrition Facts Per serving (croquettes and salad)	
Amount	
Calories	324
Fat	12 g
Sodium	440 mg
Carbohydrate	46 g
Fiber	3 g
Protein	19 g

6 servings • PREPARATION: 10 minutes • COOKING TIME: 30 minutes

METHOD

In a large saucepan, heat canola oil over high heat and sauté onion until softened.

Add all remaining ingredients and bring to a boil. Reduce heat to low and simmer, about 20 minutes, until rice is cooked.

INGREDIENTS

1 tbsp canola oil

1 small onion, chopped

1 cup (250 ml) long-grain rice

1 cup (250 ml) low-sodium beef stock

1 can (28 oz/796 ml) crushed tomatoes, no added salt

1 can (14 oz/398 ml) corn kernels, rinsed and drained

1 can (19 oz/540 ml) can black beans, rinsed and drained (see Tip)

½ cup (125 ml) water

1 tbsp dried oregano

1 tsp garlic powder

Salt and pepper

Nutrition Facts Per serving	
Amount	
Calories	310
Fat	5 g
Sodium	290 mg
Carbohydrate	60 g
Fiber	9 g
Protein	12 g

DIABETES INFO

• •

Legumes are an excellent source of fiber. They can help control blood sugar and cholesterol. You should include them regularly in your diet.

SPAGHETTI
with Ground Pork

6 servings • PREPARATION: 10 minutes • COOKING TIME: 20 minutes

INGREDIENTS

13 oz (375 g) whole wheat pasta

Canola oil

1 onion, chopped

1 lb (500 g) ground pork

2 cups (500 ml) chopped cauliflower

1 cup (250 ml) chopped celery

3 cups (750 ml) store-bought spaghetti sauce

1 tbsp basil

1 tbsp garlic powder

1 tbsp thyme

METHOD

Cook pasta in boiling water until tender.

Meanwhile, heat a bit of canola oil in a skillet over high heat and sauté onion until softened. Add ground pork.

When pork is almost cooked through, add cauliflower and celery.

In a large saucepan over medium-low heat, combine ground pork and vegetables with spaghetti sauce. Add seasonings and heat.

Combine pasta with sauce and serve.

• • • • • • • • • • • • • •

TIP

Don't like whole wheat pasta? To get used to it, start by making half regular and half whole wheat.

DIABETES INFO

• •

Whole wheat pasta is rich in fiber, making it much easier to control blood sugar than regular pasta.

Nutrition Facts Per serving	
Amount	
Calories	440
Fat	13 g
Sodium	102 mg
Carbohydrate	60 g
Fiber	8 g
Protein	25 g

SPINACH QUICHE
with Green Salad

4 servings • PREPARATION: 10 minutes • COOKING TIME: 25 minutes

INGREDIENTS

4 eggs

¾ cup (180 ml) milk

½ cup (125 ml) grated cheese

¼ cup (60 ml) unbleached
all-purpose flour

¼ cup (60 ml) whole wheat flour

1 tsp baking powder

1 tsp garlic powder

1 tbsp dried parsley

1 tbsp dried oregano

1 onion, chopped

1 red pepper, chopped

2 cups (500 ml) baby spinach

8 slices whole-grain bread

For the Green Salad

4 cups (1 l) torn romaine lettuce

1 cucumber, diced

3 tbsp vinaigrette

METHOD

Position rack in middle of oven and preheat to 300ºF (150ºC). Grease a 9-inch (23 cm) pie plate or square pan.

In a bowl, using a fork, whisk eggs and milk. Add grated cheese.

In another bowl, combine flours, baking powder, garlic powder, parsley and oregano.

Gradually combine egg mixture with dry ingredients, stirring well.

Add chopped onion, red pepper and spinach. Combine well.

Pour mixture into prepared pie plate or square pan.

Bake in middle of preheated oven for 25 minutes, until knife inserted into center comes out clean and top is golden brown. Remove from oven and let set for 5 minutes.

Slice into 4 slices.

In a bowl, combine torn romaine lettuce, cucumber and vinaigrette.

Serve quiche with salad and 2 slices whole-grain bread.

DIABETES INFO

Spinach is rich in carotenoids (lutein and zeaxanthin), antioxidants that are particularly important for eye health.

Nutrition Facts	
Per serving (quiche salade and bread)	
Amount	
Calories	440
Fat	19 g
Sodium	680 mg
Carbohydrate	45 g
Fiber	7 g
Protein	22 g

HEARTY
Beef Soup

6 servings • PREPARATION: 15 minutes • COOKING TIME: 40 to 45 minutes

INGREDIENTS

1 tbsp canola oil

1 lb (500 g) beef, cut in small cubes

1 onion, chopped

2 cloves garlic, crushed

8 cups (2 l) water

3 cups (750 ml) frozen mixed vegetables

2 carrots, cut in chunks

1 cup (250 ml) pot barley

3 tbsp beef bouillon powder

2 tbsp dried thyme

2 bay leaves

Salt and pepper

METHOD

In a large saucepan, heat canola oil over high heat and brown beef cubes, onion and garlic.

Add water, mixed vegetables, carrots, barley, beef bouillon and seasoning.

Simmer over low heat, 40 to 45 minutes, until beef is cooked through and vegetables are tender.

. . . .

TIP

This soup can be stored in an air tight container in the freezer for up to 3 months.

DIABETES INFO

The water-soluble fiber in barley is great for people with diabetes, because it slows digestion, making it easier to control blood sugar and hunger.

Nutrition Facts Per serving	
Amount	
Calories	490
Fat	11 g
Sodium	165 mg
Carbohydrate	65 g
Fiber	15 g
Protein	35 g

ASIAN Shrimp

6 servings • PREPARATION: 10 minutes • COOKING TIME: 15 minutes

METHOD

In a large skillet, heat canola oil over medium heat. Add shrimp, lemon zest and juice, broccoli, parsley, garlic powder, salt and pepper and sauté about 5 minutes until shrimp are pink and opaque.

Meanwhile, in a bowl, pour boiling water over rice noodles with chicken bouillon. Let soak for 5 minutes, then drain.

Serve shrimp and vegetables on a bed of noodles (1 cup/250 ml per person).

INGREDIENTS

1 tbsp canola oil

3½ cups (875 ml) large uncooked shrimp, shelled

Zest and juice of 1 lemon

2 cups (500 ml) broccoli pieces

1 tsp fresh chopped parsley

1 tbsp garlic powder

Salt and pepper

4 cups (1 l) boiling water

14 oz (400 g) rice noodles

1 tbsp low-sodium chicken bouillon powder

Nutrition Facts
Per serving

Amount	
Calories	370
Fat	4.5 g
Sodium	450 mg
Carbohydrate	58 g
Fiber	2 g
Protein	21 g

DIABETES INFO

Shrimp are rich in omega-3s, good fats that reduce the risk of heart disease, one of the common complications of diabetes.

SALMON
Burgers

6 burgers • PREPARATION: 15 minutes • COOKING TIME: 15 minutes

INGREDIENTS

3 cans (each 3½ oz/105 g) salmon, drained

1 cup (250 ml) breadcrumbs

2 eggs

1 tbsp Dijon mustard

1 cup (250 ml) finely grated carrots

1 tsp dried parsley

1 tbsp garlic powder

1 clove garlic, crushed

2 tbsp canola oil

6 whole-grain hamburger buns

METHOD

In a food processor or with a fork, combine all ingredients, except canola oil and buns.

Using your hands, shape mixture into 6 small patties.

In a skillet, heat canola oil over high heat and cook patties 2 to 3 minutes on each side until golden brown.

Top each hamburger bun with a patty and condiments to taste. Serve with a vegetable salad.

• • • • • • • • • • • • • •

TIP

Freeze unused patties. They make a quick, healthy meal.

Nutrition Facts Per serving	
Amount	
Calories	334
Fat	12 g
Sodium	440 mg
Carbohydrate	46 g
Fiber	3 g
Protein	19 g

ORANGE
Beef

4 servings • **PREPARATION:** 10 minutes • **COOKING TIME:** 35 minutes

INGREDIENTS

4 medium potatoes

1 lb (500 g) beef, cut in strips

½ cup (125 ml) cornstarch

3 tbsp canola oil

1 onion, chopped

4 green peppers, cut in strips

1 tbsp dried thyme

Salt and pepper

For the sauce

¼ cup (60 ml) water

Zest and juice of 2 oranges
(or ½ cup/125 ml 100%
pure orange juice)

2 tbsp sugar

2 tbsp low-sodium soy sauce

1 tbsp rice vinegar or white vinegar

1 tbsp cornstarch

METHOD

Preheat oven to 350ºF (180ºC). Bake potatoes in preheated oven for 20 minutes.

Coat beef strips in cornstarch.

In a skillet, heat canola oil over high heat. Sauté onion for 1 minute, then sear beef strips, 3 to 4 minutes on each side.

Reduce heat to medium, add peppers, thyme, salt and pepper and cook about 10 minutes.

Meanwhile, in a bowl, combine ingredients for sauce.

Pour sauce over beef and heat through.

Serve with potatoes.

Nutrition Facts Per serving	
Amount	
Calories	516
Fat	17 g
Sodium	386 mg
Carbohydrate	60 g
Fiber	4 g
Protein	18 g

MAPLE CHICKEN
Brochettes

4 servings • PREPARATION: 15 minutes • COOKING TIME: 30 minutes

INGREDIENTS

1 cup (250 ml) long-grain rice

2 large (or 4 small) boneless skinless chicken breasts, cut in pieces

10 mushrooms

2 onions, cut in large pieces

1 red pepper, cut in large pieces

1 yellow pepper, cut in large pieces

For the marinade

3 tbsp olive oil

2 tbsp Dijon mustard

1 clove garlic, crushed

2 tbsp maple syrup

1 tbsp dried thyme

Salt and pepper

METHOD

Position rack in middle of oven and preheat to 350ºF (180ºC).

Cook rice according to package directions.

In a bowl, combine ingredients for marinade.

Coat chicken in marinade and let sit, 10 to 30 minutes.

Thread brochettes on skewers, alternating chicken, mushroom, onion and pepper.

Place skewers on a baking sheet and bake in middle of preheated oven, turning occasionally, for 20 minutes, until chicken is no longer pink inside.

Serve with rice and your choice of salad.

Nutrition Facts Per serving	
Amount	
Calories	506
Fat	15 g
Sodium	186 mg
Carbohydrate	55 g
Fiber	4 g
Protein	38 g

MEXICAN SOUP
with Pita Chips

6 servings • PREPARATION: 15 minutes • COOKING TIME: 45 minutes

METHOD

In a bowl, combine ground beef, bread-crumbs and garlic powder. Press firmly with your hands to form meatballs the size of a golf ball.

Place all ingredients in a large saucepan, except meatballs and cheese, and add 2 cups (500 ml) water.

Cook over medium heat until stock is hot, then carefully add meatballs. Cook about 30 minutes, until meatballs are cooked through.

Add grated cheese right before serving.

Serve with pita chips.

Position rack in middle of oven and preheat to 350ºF (180ºC). Tear pita bread into pieces. Brush with olive oil and sprinkle with garlic powder and paprika. Bake in middle of preheated oven, 5 or 6 minutes, until crispy.

INGREDIENTS

1 lb (500 g) lean ground beef

¾ cup (180 ml) breadcrumbs

1 tbsp garlic powder

1 cup (250 ml) beef stock

1 can (28 oz/796 ml) crushed tomatoes, no salt added

1 can (5½ oz/156 ml) tomato paste

2 red peppers, chopped

1 can (14 oz/398 ml) corn kernels, drained

3 cloves garlic, chopped

1 tbsp dried thyme

A few drops hot pepper sauce

Salt and pepper

1 cup (250 ml) grated cheese

For the Pita Chips

1 large pita bread

1 tbsp olive oil

Garlic powder to taste

Paprika to taste

Nutrition Facts	
Per serving	
Amount	
Calories	469
Fat	15 g
Sodium	764 mg
Carbohydrate	55 g
Fiber	8 g
Protein	31 g

FRUITY CHICKEN
and Quinoa Salad

4 servings • PREPARATION: 10 minutes • COOKING TIME: 35 minutes

INGREDIENTS

1 cup (250 ml) uncooked quinoa

2 cups (500 ml) chicken stock

1 tbsp canola oil

1 onion, chopped

2 large (or 4 small) boneless skinless chicken breasts

1 tsp garlic powder

2 carrots, chopped

1 zucchini, chopped

1 red apple, diced

2 tbsp olive oil

1 tsp lemon juice

1 tbsp dried thyme

Salt and pepper

METHOD

Add quinoa to boiling chicken stock and reduce heat to medium. Let simmer for 20 to 25 minutes.

In a skillet, heat canola oil over high heat and sauté onion. Add chicken and garlic powder and cook until chicken is no longer pink inside.

Slice chicken into strips.

In a large bowl, combine quinoa, chicken, sautéed onion, carrots, zucchini, apple, olive oil, lemon juice, dried thyme, salt and pepper.

Refrigerate for 15 to 20 minutes before serving or serve at room temperature.

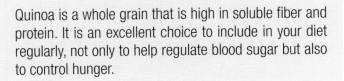

DIABETES INFO

Quinoa is a whole grain that is high in soluble fiber and protein. It is an excellent choice to include in your diet regularly, not only to help regulate blood sugar but also to control hunger.

Nutrition Facts Per serving	
Amount	
Calories	388
Fat	15 g
Sodium	486 mg
Carbohydrate	41 g
Fiber	6 g
Protein	23 g

PASTA SHELLS
with Olives, Tuna and Tomatoes

6 servings • PREPARATION: 15 minutes • COOKING TIME: 25 minutes

INGREDIENTS

2½ cups (625 ml) whole wheat pasta shells (or macaroni)

1 tbsp canola oil

1 onion, chopped

2 cloves garlic, chopped

2 cans (each 3½ oz/105 g) tuna, drained

1 cup (250 ml) black or green pitted olives, chopped

1 can (28 oz/796 ml) tomatoes with Italian spices, no salt added

1 can (5½ oz/156 ml) tomato paste

1 green pepper, chopped

1 tbsp dried basil

Black pepper to taste

½ cup (125 ml) grated cheese

METHOD

Cook pasta in boiling water until al dente.

In a skillet, heat canola oil over high heat and sauté onion and garlic. Add tuna, olives, tomatoes, tomato paste, green pepper, basil and pepper. Heat for about 10 minutes.

In a large saucepan or salad bowl, combine pasta with tuna mixture and top with grated cheese.

Nutrition Facts Per serving	
Amount	
Calories	372
Fat	12 g
Sodium	830 mg
Carbohydrate	52 g
Fiber	8 g
Protein	20 g

EGG
Burgers

4 servings • PREPARATION: 15 minutes • COOKING TIME: 7 minutes

METHOD

Cook eggs in boiling water for 7 minutes until hard-boiled.

Run cooked eggs under cold water and peel them.

In a large bowl, using a fork, mash eggs coarsely with mayonnaise, yogurt, green onion and seasonings.

Toast hamburger buns and melt cheese on top of one half under the broiler. Top with egg mixture, and 1 lettuce leaf.

Serve with salad or raw vegetables.

INGREDIENTS

6 eggs

1 tbsp light mayonnaise

2 tbsp plain yogurt

1 green onion, chopped

1 tbsp garlic powder

1 tbsp paprika

Salt and pepper

4 whole-grain hamburger buns

4 slices cheese

4 lettuce leaves

DIABETES INFO

Eggs are a good source of protein and replace a serving of meat. The protein in eggs helps manage blood sugar and control hunger.

Nutrition Facts
Per serving

Amount	
Calories	315
Fat	15 g
Sodium	475 mg
Carbohydrate	27 g
Fiber	2 g
Protein	19 g

BREADED PORK CHOPS
with Vegetable Pasta

4 servings • **PREPARATION:** 10 minutes • **COOKING TIME:** 10 minutes

INGREDIENTS

1 egg

2 tbsp Dijon mustard

1 cup (250 ml) ground almonds

6 tbsp unbleached all-purpose flour, divided

1 tsp garlic powder

1 tsp dried thyme

Salt and pepper

1 tbsp canola oil

4 large or 8 small pork chops

For the Vegetable Pasta

2 cups (500 ml) cooked whole wheat pasta

2 carrots, chopped

1 cup (250 ml) broccoli pieces

2 peppers, chopped

2 tbsp olive oil

1 tbsp lemon juice

Salt and pepper to taste

METHOD

In a bowl, beat egg and Dijon mustard.

In another bowl, combine almonds, 2 tbsp flour and seasonings.

In a third bowl, place 4 tbsp flour. Dredge pork chops in flour.

Dip floury pork chops in beaten egg and then in almond mixture, coating well.

In a skillet, heat canola oil over medium-high heat and cook pork chops for 3 to 5 minutes on each side. Serve with vegetable pasta.

In a large bowl, combine cooked whole wheat pasta, carrots, broccoli, peppers, olive oil, lemon juice, salt and pepper.

• • • • • • • • • • • • • •

VARIATION

Replace almonds with 1 cup (250 ml) ground corn cereal such as Corn Flakes or 1 cup (250 ml) breadcrumbs.

Nutrition Facts Per serving	
Amount	
Calories	334
Fat	12 g
Sodium	440 mg
Carbohydrate	46 g
Fiber	3 g
Protein	19 g

SOLE
en Papillote

4 servings • PREPARATION: 10 minutes • COOKING TIME: 20 minutes

INGREDIENTS

1½ cups (375 ml) long-grain rice

2 cups (500 ml) water

1 tbsp low-sodium chicken bouillon powder

1 tbsp dried thyme

4 sole fillets

1 tbsp dried basil

1 cup (250 ml) chopped celery

1 red pepper, chopped

1 small onion, chopped

2 cups (500 ml) cauliflower florets

Black pepper

1 tbsp lemon juice

METHOD

Position rack in middle of oven and preheat to 350ºF (180ºC).

Cook rice in a saucepan with water, chicken bouillon and thyme according to package directions, about 20 minutes.

Place each sole fillet on a sheet of aluminum foil and sprinkle with dried basil. Distribute celery, red pepper, onion and cauliflower around fillets. Sprinkle with black pepper and fold aluminum foil into packets.

Bake in middle of preheated oven for 15 minutes.

Drizzle lemon juice over cooked sole, sprinkle with pepper and serve each portion with 1 cup (250 ml) rice.

Nutrition Facts	
Per serving	
Amount	
Calories	440
Fat	3 g
Sodium	448 mg
Carbohydrate	63 g
Fiber	3 g
Protein	37 g

PITA
Pizza

4 servings • PREPARATION: 15 minutes • COOKING TIME: 10 minutes

INGREDIENTS

⅓ cup (80 ml) tomato paste

2 tsp olive oil

1 tbsp dried basil

Salt and pepper

4 whole wheat pitas

2 small boneless skinless chicken breasts, cooked and cut in pieces

2 peppers, cut in strips

1 cup (250 ml) grated cheese

METHOD

Position rack in middle of oven and preheat to 350ºF (180ºC).

In a bowl, combine tomato paste with olive oil and basil. Season with salt and pepper.

Brush pita bread with tomato paste mixture.

Top pita with chicken, peppers and cheese.

Bake in middle of preheated oven, 5 to 10 minutes, until cheese is melted.

Serve with a green salad.

• • • • • • • • • • • • • •

TIP

To have pita pizzas on hand whenever you need them, freeze before baking.

Nutrition Facts Per serving	
Amount	
Calories	423
Fat	15 g
Sodium	587 mg
Carbohydrate	45 g
Fiber	6 g
Protein	30 g

BLUEBERRY ✓
Muffins

12 muffins • PREPARATION: 10 minutes • COOKING TIME: 20 to 25 minutes

INGREDIENTS

1 cup (250 ml) unbleached all-purpose flour

1 cup (250 ml) quick-cooking rolled oats

¼ cup (60 ml) oat bran

2 tsp baking powder

¼ cup (60 ml) canola oil

¼ cup (60 ml) sugar

2 eggs

¾ cup (180 ml) milk

1½ cups (375 ml) frozen blueberries

METHOD

Position rack in middle of oven and preheat to 350°F (180°C). Lightly grease muffin tin or line with paper liners.

In a bowl, combine flour, oats, oat bran and baking powder.

In another bowl, beat canola oil, sugar and eggs for 2 minutes. Gradually add milk while beating.

Pour wet ingredients over dry ingredients, combining well. Add frozen blueberries.

Pour mixture into prepared muffin tin and bake in middle of preheated oven 20 to 25 minutes.

• • • • • • • • • • • • • •

TIP

Prepare muffins when you have free time and freeze them in a freezer bag. When you want a muffin, microwave for 15 seconds or defrost in the fridge.

Nutrition Facts
Per serving

Amount	
Calories	158
Fat	6 g
Sodium	70 mg
Carbohydrate	23 g
Fiber	2 g
Protein	4.6 g

ORANGE
Tapioca

8 servings of ½ cup (125 ml) • PREPARATION: 5 minutes • COOKING TIME: 10 to 15 minutes

INGREDIENTS

¾ cup (180 ml) medium pearl tapioca

3 cups (750 ml) milk

1 tsp vanilla

1 cup (250 ml) 100% pure orange juice

1 tbsp white sugar

METHOD

In a saucepan, heat tapioca, milk, vanilla, orange juice and sugar over low heat.

Simmer until thickened, about 10 to 15 minutes.

Let cool. Enjoy cold or at room temperature.

DIABETES INFO

• •

100% pure fruit juice, even if it has no added sugar, has sugar that is quickly absorbed, which in turn quickly increases blood sugar. It's best to avoid fruit juice in the morning and evening if your blood sugar is hard to control. And it is a good idea not to drink more than 1 cup (250 ml) of juice a day, which equals two servings of fruit.

Nutrition Facts Per serving	
Amount	
Calories	79
Fat	1 g
Sodium	40 mg
Carbohydrate	14 g
Fiber	0 g
Protein	4 g

PEACH
Crisp

10 servings • PREPARATION: 10 minutes • COOKING TIME: 20 minutes

METHOD

Preheat oven to 350ºF (180ºC).

In a bowl, combine oats, flour, almonds and brown sugar.

Stir in eggs and margarine.

In an ovenproof dish, spread peaches and top with oats. Distribute evenly.

Bake in preheated oven for 20 minutes.

• • • • • • • • • • • • • •

VARIATIONS

- This recipe can be made with pears, apples, berries, rhubarb, nectarines, cherries or pineapple. Frozen or properly drained canned fruit can be a good replacement for fresh fruit.

- If you don't have flaked almonds, omit them or replace them with another sort of nut.

INGREDIENTS

2 cups (500 ml) old-fashioned rolled oats

¼ cup (60 ml) whole wheat flour

½ cup (125 ml) flaked almonds or other chopped nuts

¼ cup (60 ml) brown sugar

2 eggs, beaten

2 tbsp melted non-hydrogenated margarine

3 cups (750 ml) chopped fresh peaches (or canned peaches, drained)

DIABETES INFO

Almonds are rich in nutrients, fiber, protein and antioxidants. Eating them daily reduces blood LDL (bad) cholesterol and helps control blood sugar. A small handful of almonds daily as a snack or at meals is a healthy choice.

Nutrition Facts Per serving	
Amount	
Calories	165
Fat	46 g
Sodium	32 mg
Carbohydrate	23 g
Fiber	3 g
Protein	5 g

OATMEAL DATE
Cookies

25 cookies • PREPARATION: 10 minutes • COOKING TIME: 25 minutes

INGREDIENTS

2 cups (500 ml) dried dates

2 cups (500 ml) water

2 cups (500 ml) quick-cooking rolled oats

1 cup (250 ml) whole wheat flour

1 tsp baking powder

2 eggs

¼ cup (60 ml) brown sugar

1 cup (250 ml) milk

METHOD

Position rack in middle of oven and preheat to 350ºF (180ºC). Line a baking sheet with parchment paper or grease.

In a saucepan over medium-high heat, cook dates in water for about 15 minutes, until water evaporates. Once dates are cooked, mash them with a fork.

In a bowl, combine oats, flour and baking powder.

In a mixer, beat eggs with brown sugar. Gradually pour in milk. Then add date purée with a spoon.

Pour wet mixture over dry ingredients. Mix thoroughly.

Using an ice cream scoop, place dough onto prepared baking sheet. Bake in middle of preheated oven for 10 minutes.

Nutrition Facts Per cookie	
Amount	
Calories	83
Fat	1 g
Sodium	24 mg
Carbohydrate	17 g
Fiber	2 g
Protein	3 g

LEMON
Pudding

6 servings • PREPARATION: 5 minutes • COOKING TIME: 6 to 7 minutes

INGREDIENTS

2 cups (500 ml) milk

2 tbsp cornstarch

¼ cup (60 ml) white sugar

½ cup (125 ml) fresh lemon juice

METHOD

In a saucepan, combine milk, cornstarch and sugar. Cook over medium heat, stirring constantly.

Allow pudding to thicken, about 6 to 7 minutes. Once thickened, add lemon juice and stir well.

Pour into six ⅔ cup (160 ml) ramekins and refrigerate.

Nutrition Facts Per serving	
Amount	
Calories	85
Fat	0.8 g
Sodium	40 mg
Carbohydrate	17 g
Fiber	0 g
Protein	3 g

ABOUT
the Author

Alexandra Leduc is a registered dietitian, who graduated in biochemistry and nutrition from Laval University. She is the author of many cookbooks.

She is also the founder of Alex Cuisine (alexcuisine.com), a company that promotes health through healthy and fast cooking. In her classes, which include parent and child coaching and online videos, she presents simple approaches to everyday cooking.

What she loves most is creating delicious recipes with readily available ingredients. "You don't need to raid an organic food store or be a great chef to eat properly," she believes. Alexandra advocates an approach to cooking that is grounded in reality and is a long way from culinary competitions.

She also offers expertise in weight management and helps people develop a healthy relationship with food and achieve a balanced weight, while avoiding diets and restrictions. She has developed an approach – mindful eating – along with an online program (alimentationconsciente.com), which presents tools for applying it daily.

In 2011, she was named Young Business Personality in the professional services category by the Jeune chambre de commerce de Québec (Young Chamber of Commerce of Quebec). In May 2013, she received the Young Woman of the Year award as part of the YWCA Quebec's Women of Distinction gala, and in 2014, Laval University's Alumni Association named her Influential Alumnus.

alexcuisine.com

ACKNOWLEDGMENTS

I want to thank my husband and my family who make it possible for me to do what I do. Your unconditional support and encouragement mean so much to me.

Thank you to three of the best colleagues and nutritionists one could ask for, Laurie Parent-Drolet, Marie-Pier Tremblay and Alexandra Morneau. You cheerfully tested the recipes and guided me with your clinical experience and helpful comments.

A special thanks to Groupe Modus, Marc G. Alain and Isabelle Jodoin for your trust and for the great projects you allow me to be part of; you make it such a good experience. Thanks for your work helping people eat better. Thanks as well to editorial assistant Nolwenn Gouezel for her tips and suggestions, and graphic designers Émilie Houle and Gabrielle Lecomte for the beautiful layout.

I must also mention the work of photographer André Noël, whose magnificent photos whet the appetite.

Finally, I would like to dedicate this book to Alexandra. This book is for you and Claire, the brightest star shining down on us.

RESOURCES
for Diabetes Sufferers

U.S.
American Association of Diabetes Educators (AADE)
www.diabeteseducator.org

American Diabetes Association (ADA)
www.diabetes.org

CANADA
Canadian Diabetes Association (CDA)
www.diabetes.ca

Diabète Québec (DQ)
www.diabete.qc.ca

The Diabetic Children's Foundation
www.diabetes-children.ca

U.K.
Diabetes UK
www.diabetes.org.uk

AUSTRALIA
Diabetes Australia
www.diabetesaustralia.com.au

RECIPE Index

KNOW WHAT TO EAT

A diet suited to your needs based on advice from expert dietitians

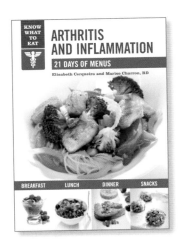

KNOW WHAT TO EAT

ARTHRITIS AND INFLAMMATION

21 DAYS OF MENUS

Elisabeth Cerqueira and Marise Charron, RD

BREAKFAST · LUNCH · DINNER · SNACKS

KNOW WHAT TO EAT

SPORTS NUTRITION

21 DAYS OF MENUS

Stéphanie Côté and Philippe Grand, RD

BREAKFAST · LUNCH · DINNER · SNACKS

KNOW WHAT TO EAT

DIABETES

21 DAYS OF MENUS

Alexandra Leduc, RD

BREAKFAST · LUNCH · DINNER · SNACKS

KNOW WHAT TO EAT

WEIGHT LOSS

21 DAYS OF MENUS

Elisabeth Cerqueira and Marise Charron, RD

BREAKFAST · LUNCH · DINNER · SNACKS

MODUSVIVENDIPUBLISHING.COM